✸ This books belongs to ✸

....

....

....

Indian Elephant Mandala

Circular mandala isolated

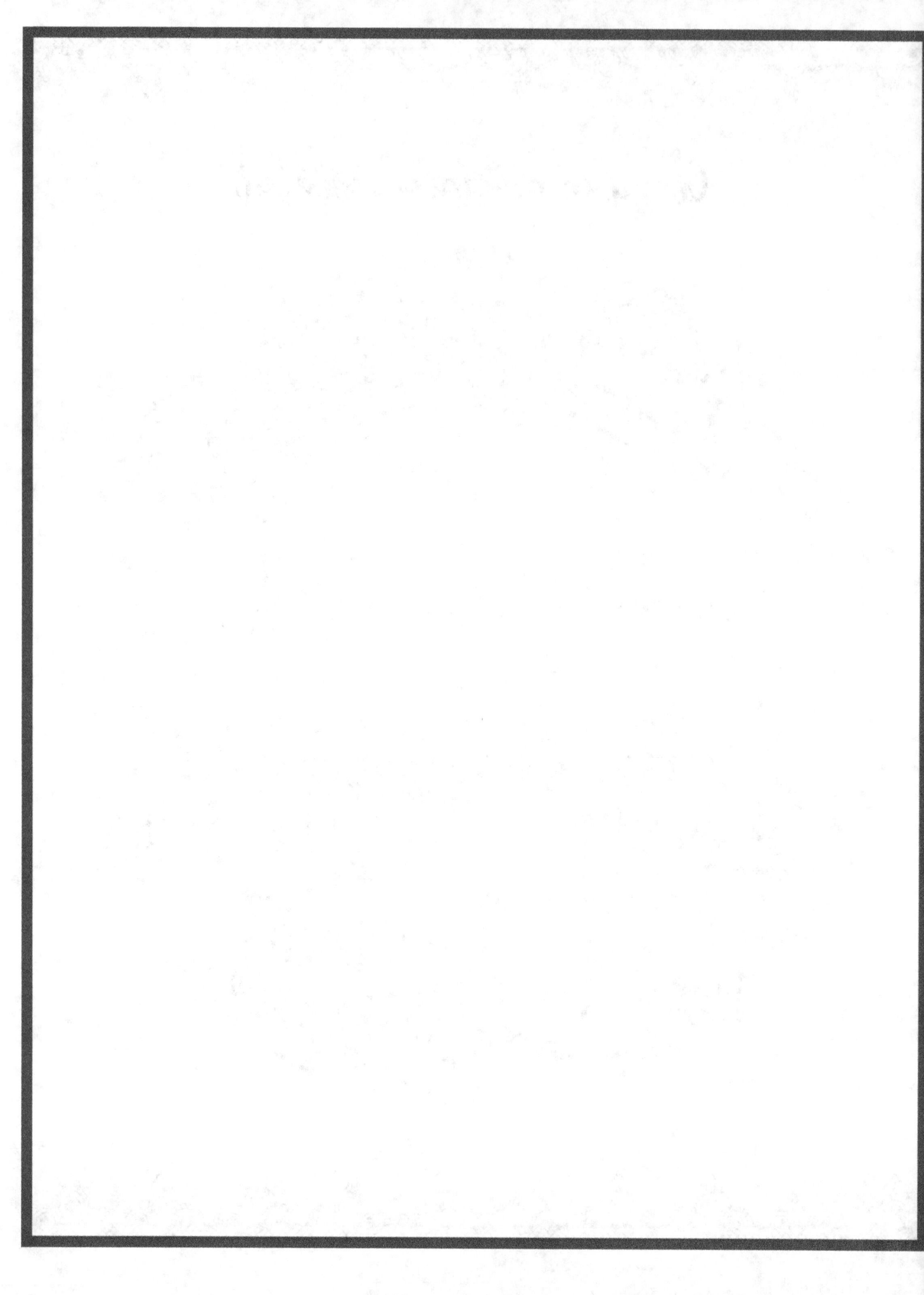

Oriental therapy yoga mandalas

Oriental therapy yoga mandalas

Luxury arabesque mandala

Indian Elephant Mandala

Indian Elephant Mandala

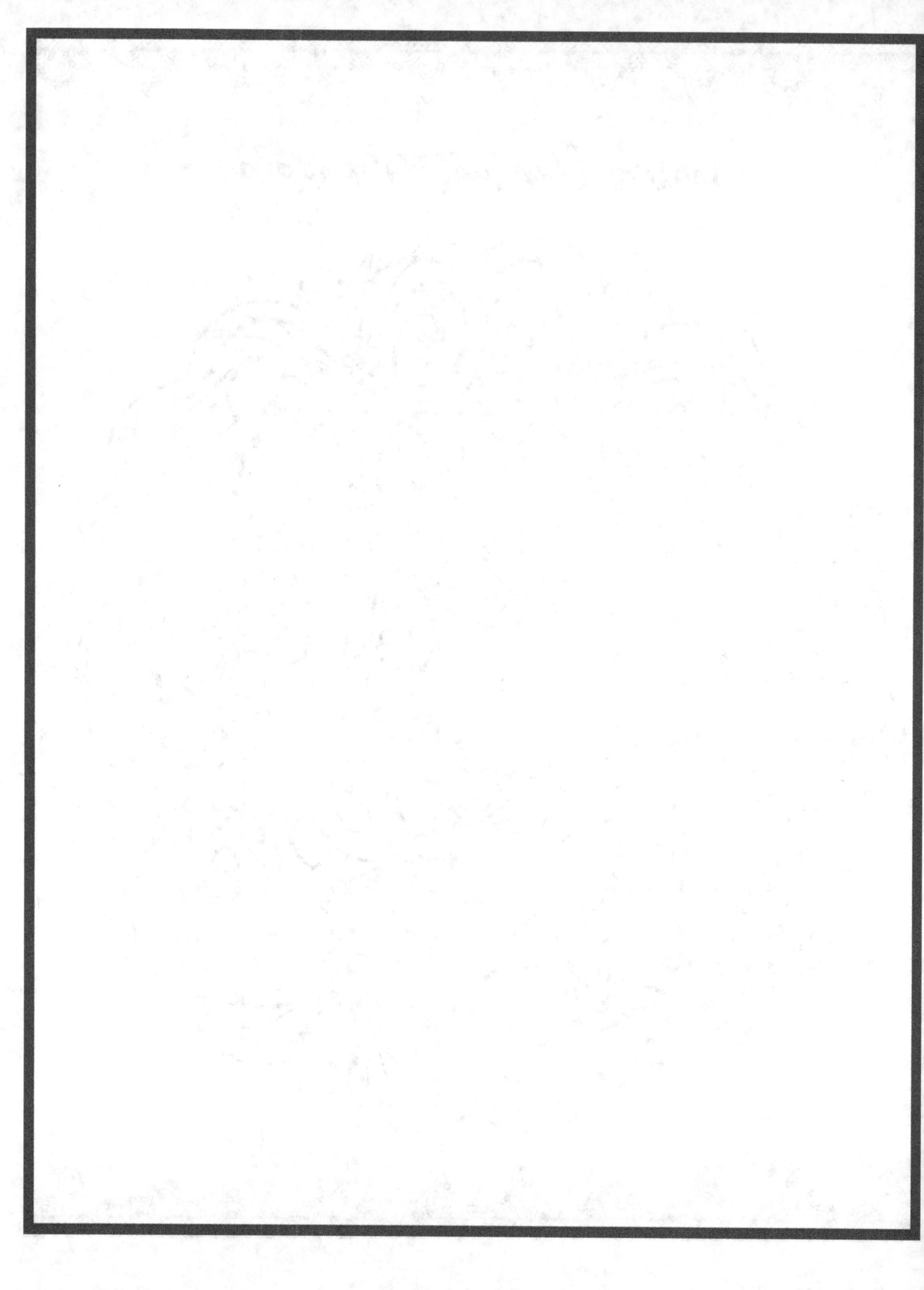

Ethnic fractal mandala meditation

Floral Mandalas

Circle shape pattern with cute birds Mandalas

Floral Mandalas

Floral Mandalas

Circular symmetric mandala

Circular symmetric mandala

Circular symmetric mandala

Circular symmetric mandala

Circular symmetric mandala

Circular symmetric mandala

Circular symmetric mandala

Circular symmetric mandala

Circular symmetric mandala

Macaw mandala zentangle and tshirt

Butterfly mandala

Butterfly mandala

www.ingramcontent.com/pod-product-compliance
Lightning Source LLC
Chambersburg PA
CBHW081546220526
45467CB00010B/3347